Masters of Persuasion

Secrets to Convincing People

Dear reader,

We want to know what you think. After reading this, visit our website www.ebooktop.com.br register and contribute with suggestions, criticisms or compliments.

Have a good read!

Copyright

Copyright © 2024 de Buenos Livros

All rights reserved. This ebook or any part of it may not be reproduced or used in any way without the express written permission of the author or publisher, except for the use of brief quotations in a review.

First edition 2024.

www.ebooktop.com.br

What is PERSUASION?

Persuasion is the process of influencing other people's attitudes, beliefs, behaviors or decisions through argumentation, effective communication and persuasive techniques. It involves the ability to present arguments convincingly, appealing to emotions, values, logic or authority, in order to motivate others to agree with a particular point of view, take a particular action or adopt an idea. Persuasion is an important skill in many areas of life, such as negotiations, sales, politics, advertising and interpersonal relationships.

CONTENTS

Introduction	8
Chapter 1 - Mental Triggers	15
Chapter 2 - Overview of a persuasive text or sales letter.	20
Chapter 3 - Basic elements of a sales letter - Questions and Answers	27
Chapter 4 - Scoring the most important tips for writing a sales letter	39
Chapter 5 - Do aesthetics matter for your sales letter?	51
Chapter 6 - Why do certain sales letters lose business?	60
Chapter 7 - What are the fatal mistakes in email marketing?	65
Chapter 8 - What are the pitfalls of a "what if" approach?	69
Chapter 9 - What do you do when you just can't write a sales letter?	73
Chapter 10 - The difference between a sales letter and an advertisement	77
Chapter 11 - Does a text need to be long or short to be persuasive?	85
Chapter 12 - The ten basic rules for writing a good sales letter	95
Chapter 13 - Five useful secrets of an effective sales letter	97
Chapter 14 - Final Summary	105

Introduction

What you'll learn in this book won't just help you send well-written emails. But you will learn the art of persuasion. This will be useful in your life as a professional. As well as persuasive texts, you'll be able to use these techniques to meet clients and talk to them face-to-face. Knowing how to use mental triggers and break down objections is essential for any salesperson to stand out in their company.

Foreword

The main objective of every company is to be valued by its customers. To try to increase their importance among customers, companies need to use marketing tools.

But the first step before using these tools, the basic thing you need to understand is what makes your business tick. Without this knowledge, it doesn't matter whether you use Google ads or social media, you're unlikely to get good results.

You need to set clear objectives and realistic targets to start working on your company's marketing. That's why we like to talk about persuasive texts and sales letters. When preparing a persuasive text, you'll need to go through steps that will help you clearly define these objectives.

We're going to teach you rhetorical questions that will help you clearly define what kind of actions you want to get from your client.

Sales letters, or email marketings, are widely used communication tools. They warm up the customer and create a bond with you. What's more, they can help build your customer base and increase your sales.

> ❖ *In some publications, the term "lead" is also used to refer to potential customers.*

Some questions we will answer in this book:

- What makes marketing emails always get read?
- What makes them sell products?
- What is the secret that keeps readers reading until the end?
- Why do some sales letters manage to convince us to buy, while others don't, even if they offer the same benefits and features?

Sales letters can contain different types of information. For example:

a) They inform you about the products and services you offer. The main reason for using sales letters as a marketing tool is to inform customers about what you sell by providing facts that grab the reader's attention.

b) They help to schedule future meetings, *lives* or courses. Sales letters can be used to make these invitations to customers, whether for a personal visit, a call or a *live stream*.

c) They answer questions. If a customer has previously asked questions about a specific product or service, a sales letter can be sent to answer those questions and possibly make a sale.

d) They provide general information. A sales letter can inform customers about new offers, products, services, sales, etc. It can be any information that you find interesting to the reader, either at the customer's request or as part of a marketing strategy.

To write an effective sales letter, it's important to define your objectives. Once your objective is clear, it will be easier to decide which technique to use.

Here are some common goals:

a) Sell a product or service. If you want to convince people to buy what you sell, you need to use persuasive words, but without being aggressive. Keep a conversational tone.

b) Inform the customer. If your aim is to provide all the essential information about your company, product or service, you can accompany the sales letter with leaflets or other inserts.

c) Getting a response. Customers may contact you for different reasons apart from buying. It could be for more information, a free sample, a personal visit, etc. Keep the option open to demonstrate the product or service, this helps to build credibility.

Writing an effective sales letter isn't as difficult as it sounds. Sure, you may need to learn some new skills, but all the great sales letter writers started from scratch. With persistence and practice, you too can write sales letters that sell.

This book will guide you step by step through the process of writing an effective sales letter. From defining your objective to the basic elements of a sales letter and valuable tips for increasing your sales, you'll find it all in this book.

- ❖ *When we use the expressions "sales letters" or "persuasive texts" we are referring to marketing emails, web sales pages, copy or any written information that you want to use to convince someone to take action.*

What you'll learn in this book won't just help you send well-written emails. But you will learn the art of persuasion. This will be useful in your life as a professional. As well as persuasive texts, you'll be able to use these techniques to meet clients and talk to them face-to-face. Knowing how to use mental triggers and break down objections is essential for any salesperson to stand out in their company.

Chapter 1 - Mental Triggers

You can't understand persuasive texts without first studying and clearly understanding what mental triggers are.

Mental triggers are stimuli that activate emotional or psychological impulses in a person, leading them to take a certain action, such as buying a product, making a decision or changing their behavior. These triggers exploit common patterns of human thought and behavior, taking advantage of aspects such as curiosity, urgency, authority, reciprocity, among others. They are often used in marketing, sales, persuasion and communication to subtly and effectively influence people's decisions.

In the complex web of human psychology, mental triggers are powerful tools for influencing decisions and shaping behavior. From marketing strategies to social interactions, understanding these triggers is essential for anyone looking to positively impact the choices of others. In this article, we'll explore different types of mental triggers, analyzing their applications and the psychological principles behind each one.

1. Scarcity: The Fear of Missing Out

The scarcity mental trigger exploits the human fear of missing out on opportunities. When something is presented as limited in quantity or time, the perception of value increases dramatically. Promoting a product as "limited edition" or "last units available" activates the instinct of urgency in people, leading them to act to secure what may be about to disappear.

2. Social Proof: The Power of Social Validation

The human tendency to follow the behavior of others is the basis of the mental trigger of social proof. When people see other individuals doing something, especially if they are similar to them, they are more likely to follow suit. Testimonials from satisfied customers, positive reviews and numbers of followers on social networks are all forms of social proof that can influence people's decisions.

3. Authority: The Power of Knowledge and Experience

The mental trigger of authority exploits the respect and trust that people have in authority figures or experts on a particular subject. Presenting information backed up by reliable sources, such as renowned experts or scientific studies, can persuade others to accept an idea or make a decision.

4. Reciprocity: The Law of Return

The mental trigger of reciprocity is based on the idea that people tend to return favors and positive gestures. By offering something of value without expecting anything in return, you create a sense of obligation in the other person, who is more likely to respond positively in the future. This can be seen in strategies such as free samples, gifts or acts of generosity.

5. Membership: The Need to Be Part of a Tribe

The mental trigger of affiliation exploits the fundamental human desire to belong to a group or community. By highlighting the emotional connection that a product, service or idea provides, a powerful bond is created with people who want to be part of that group. Brands often use this technique in marketing campaigns that emphasize the identity and lifestyle associated with their products.

6. New: The Fascination for the Unpublished

The novelty mental trigger capitalizes on the innate human interest in new and stimulating experiences. The presentation of something unique, innovative or exclusive arouses curiosity and the desire to explore.

The constant search for novelty drives the adoption of new technologies, products and ideas, making this trigger a powerful tool for companies looking to stand out in competitive markets.

Mental triggers are fundamental tools for influencing decisions and behavior. By understanding the psychological principles behind each trigger, we can apply them ethically and effectively in various areas, from marketing and sales to interpersonal relationships. However, it is important to remember that the use of these techniques must be transparent and respect the values and interests of the people involved.

Chapter 2 - Overview of a persuasive text or sales letter.

We often talk about persuasive text here. But do you know what persuasion is? It's important to know, so let's get to it.

Persuasion is the process of influencing other people's attitudes, beliefs, behaviors or decisions through argumentation, effective communication and persuasive techniques. It involves the ability to present arguments convincingly, appealing to emotions, values, logic or authority, in order to motivate others to agree with a particular point of view, take a particular action or adopt an idea. Persuasion is an important skill in many areas of life, such as negotiations, sales, politics, advertising and interpersonal relationships.

A sales letter is a document that aims to sell something. It needs to be persuasive in order to convince the reader to place an order or request information about a product or service, or simply to click on a link. The main objective is to motivate the reader to act. That's why we call it persuasive text.

To begin with, let's look at a real example of a bad sales letter:

Subject: Results of my research and development

Body of the email: "I'm bringing you to let you know about the really amazing washing machine I've developed. First of all, I know it's wonderful because I spent years studying washing machines of all kinds. Then I broadened my field of research and development (R&D) to include all types of commercial washing machines and learned all the possible secrets of what makes dirt come out of the most inconceivable places. Now, ten years later, I'm ready to let you taste the fruits of all my hard work. I have developed EZ WASHER. I have to say that it will make all the other washing machines you've ever seen pale in comparison to mine.

Bad, right? We've identified some problems with this letter:

1. The headline focuses on the writer, not the customer.
2. Technical terms like "R&D" can confuse the customer.
3. It's not clear what the customer will receive or what the benefits of the product are.

Before writing a sales letter, it's important to put yourself in the customer's shoes. Think about how you react to advertising emails that you receive without asking. They often end up in junk mail or spam without being read. Isn't it true that most emails like this we delete without reading?

Don't worry, we'll teach you how to write email subject lines, headlines, that grab the reader's attention.

First, let's understand the difference between unsolicited proposals, brochures and sales letters.

When creating a brochure, an unsolicited proposal or a sales letter, it's useful to understand the similarities and differences between them.

- **Brochures:** These are records of products and services, usually produced on a large scale and distributed anonymously. They can contain information in different formats and not necessarily in vibrant colors.

- **Unsolicited proposals:** These are physical or digital documents about products and services, often drawn up independently and aimed at a specific, even unfamiliar, audience. They can take the form of a letter, bound documents or digital files such as a PDF.

- **Sales letters:** These are short, direct proposals aimed at motivating the reader to take action. They can be directed at specific individuals or sent to unknown people.

In practice, there isn't much difference between them. They all provide information and seek to influence the reader. However, it is important that brochures and unsolicited offers are convincing and lead the reader to take action.

Segmentation, resources and benefits

To prepare an effective sales letter, it is crucial to understand the product or service on offer, the market and the reader's needs. This includes differentiating between features and benefits.

- Features: These are the characteristics of the product or service.
- Benefits: These are the advantages that the customer gets from using the product or service.

The sales letter must emphasize the benefits in order to convince the reader to buy. In addition, it is important to consider the means of dissemination, the target audience, the competition and marketing strategies.

By understanding customers' emotional needs and how your offer can satisfy them, you'll be better placed to create an effective sales letter.

Following the **AIDA** model

Advertising copywriters follow the AIDA model, which stands for Attention, Interest, Desire and Action.

1. **ATTENTION** - Get your reader's attention.
Start your sales letter with an impactful headline or an interesting question to capture the reader's attention. For example, "Want to reduce your electricity costs by 45%?" or "Lose 5 kg in 2 weeks without starving!"

2. **INTEREST** - Gain your interest

Immediately explain to the reader why they should be interested in your product or service. Show how their life can improve with what you are offering and provide proof of your reliability, such as testimonials from satisfied customers.

3. **DESIRE** - Create desire

After attracting attention and arousing interest, create a desire for your product. Show the reader how they will benefit from what you are offering, relating the benefits to their daily lives. Use specific examples to make the offer more convincing.

4. **ACTION** - Request an action

Finally, ask the reader to take a specific action, such as filling in a response card, placing an order or calling for more information. Be sure to clearly indicate what the next step is and include a PS to reinforce the benefits or guarantees of the offer.

Chapter 3 - Basic elements of a sales letter - Questions and Answers

What are the basic parts of a sales letter? Every sales letter generally follows this sequence:

1. **Image:** Only use the company logo or design if it is relevant to what is being offered. The image should be related to the title, content and theme of the letter.
2. **Title: This** should be catchy and contain between 3 and 30 words. Its purpose is to attract the reader's attention and communicate the essence of the offer.
3. **Greeting and Lead:** Start the letter with a greeting and a lead that connects the reader to the content. This could be a quote, an interesting question or the identification of a problem that your offer solves.
4. **Body of the letter:** Keep the same tone as the title and highlight the benefits of the offer. Give details of the benefits and features, as well as creating credibility. The

aim is to arouse the need or desire for the product or service.

5. **Closing or Call to Action (CTA):** End the letter with a specific request to the reader, making it easy for them to respond. Provide means of contact, such as a pre-paid envelope, an order form, a free phone number or an email link.

Thank the reader and include a postscript to reinforce the message.

ADDITIONAL TIP: Test your text with readers to ensure its effectiveness and adjust as necessary to maximize impact.

How do you create attention-grabbing headlines for your email marketing? Every marketing tool needs a strong headline to grab the reader's attention, convey your message and encourage them to make a purchase. Here are some tips for creating impactful headlines:

1. Ask a question: "Worried about gaining weight? Find out how to lose 15 kilos in 3 weeks."
2. Start with "How": "How to lose 15 kilos in 3 weeks."
3. Use testimonials: "Satisfied customer: 'I lost 15 kilos in 3 weeks!' Find out how you can too!"
4. Issue a command: "Lose weight now! Learn the proven method in just 3 weeks."
5. Significant news: "Revolutionary new weight loss method now available!"
6. Last chance: "Special offer: save money now!"
7. Free offers: "Get a special bonus when you buy today!"

Remember, headlines should be clear, direct and relevant to the reader. They help readers decide whether they want to read more or not, so focus on capturing their attention quickly and effectively.

Is it important to have a strong first paragraph? Yes, the first paragraph is crucial to attracting the reader's attention and arousing their interest in what you're offering. Here are some tips to ensure that your first paragraph is effective:

1. Be theatrical and interesting: Capture the reader's attention with a creative and engaging approach.
2. Target the audience: Make sure your opening paragraph resonates with the audience you are trying to reach.
3. Be concise and precise: Keep the paragraph short and to the point to avoid losing the reader's interest.
4. Use "you": Involve the reader by using language directed at them, making the message more personal and engaging.
5. Avoid the third person: Starting with "we" can alienate the reader, so focus on the first person for a more direct connection.

When evaluating the first paragraph of your sales letter, check that it meets these guidelines to ensure that it is creating immediate interest and engagement with the reader. There is no strict formula for an opening paragraph, but your letters will create improved responses if you follow, rather than break, the rules.

Is it essential to include a PS in your sales letter? People like to know who sent the letter and tend to scroll quickly to the end to see the signature. Below the signature is a Postscript (or PS). In fact, your PS may be the second (after the headline) or third (after the opening sentence / paragraph) most read in your sales letter or email. Most copywriters use not just one postscript, but several (PPS).

Most PS tend to be quite short, usually around 3 or 4 lines, to summarize the offer, corroborate the deadline and include the call to action.

Webster's defines PS this way: "Postscript - Written afterward; a paragraph added to a letter after its completion and signing by the writer; an addition made to a letter or composition after the completion of the main body of the work, containing something omitted or something new occurring to the writer."

For marketers, it offers a final opportunity to influence potential customers into action. The best way to use your final "add-on" is to highlight or expose a main point of importance to the reader.

Employ these tactics. The PS is one of the most read elements of any sales letter. It ranks second only to headings and subheadings in terms of reading priority.

Keep it concise and precise. A succinct summary is enough to hold the reader's interest. If you need more space, create a secondary PS. Adding supplementary PS is a particularly effective strategy with longer sales letters.

Should you include guarantees? If you offer a product or service without a guarantee, you could be about to lose a large percentage of potential sales. Nowadays, scams are widespread. As there are no police or official moderators on the Internet, these scams are likely to be even bigger as a consequence.

Because of these scammers and the large number of challenges presented on the web, people are suspicious and increasingly looking for more protected ways to take advantage of offers. Guarantees are therefore influential tools for the opulence-seeking professional and can do two very vital things that will help increase profits: increase sales and reduce returns.

When you offer a guarantee, you reduce the cynicism surrounding the purchase of your product or service. Consumers are reasonably careful, and even more so when shopping online. And guarantees give you almost immediate trust with potential customers.

Guarantees increase perceived value. Take, for example, the story of the Monaghan brothers.

Both brothers were in a basic business. They needed money to pay for college. They worked shifts and attended college when they were free on the other shift. After suffering losses for about a year, one of the brothers sold his share of the business. The other stuck with the small pizzeria. In some interviews he gave recently, Tom Monaghan said he wasn't too sure he was doing the right thing. The rest is history. His decision was the best he ever made. His business, based on a simple guarantee, "Pizza delivered in 30 minutes or it's free", Domino's Pizza has become the billion dollar industry it is today.

Guarantees increase sales and reduce returns. When people shop, especially online, offering a hassle-free return policy increases convenience and boosts buyer confidence. So use guarantees to ensure success.

Seven tips for an optimal guarantee:

1. Make warranty easy and hassle-free. Eliminate excuses and fine print.
2. Make sure that your entire organization is aligned with the operational philosophy surrounding the use of guarantees.
3. Know your customers well enough to understand how the guarantee can benefit them.
4. Make the guarantee a two-way street; offer benefits if performance exceeds expectations and ask for "success" fees.
5. Specify which customers can make use of the guarantee and limit the number to the minimum necessary.

6. Respond quickly to customer requests for warranty compliance.
7. Monitor your performance to avoid surprises.

The guarantees fall into five different categories:

1. Money-back guarantee: Protects customers against loss of time and money, as well as covering product faults or breakages.
2. Satisfaction guarantee: Guarantees the customer's happiness and satisfaction with the service or product.
3. Price protection guarantee: Offers a fixed price and guarantees that there will be no changes or increases in price or payment terms.
4. On-time guarantee: Helps to reassure customers who are worried about the weather, and is attractive to companies such as printers, car repair shops and cable companies.

5. No-questions-asked guarantee: It works for practically anything. Just try it and see.

Chapter 4 - Scoring the most important tips for writing a sales letter

In this chapter we will present in a well-organized and summarized way important points and tips for writing your persuasive text.

10 fundamental tips for effective writing:

1. **Credibility: As** well as talking about the benefits, use testimonials from satisfied customers to show confidence in your product or service.
2. **Make it memorable:** Make your letter stand out by offering something unique, such as useful tips related to your business.
3. **Emphasize aesthetics:** Make it easy to read with an attractive design and a clear structure.
4. **Include a call to action:** Provide a means for the reader to respond, such as a postcard or order form.

5. **Offer a temptation:** Include an incentive to act immediately, such as a discount or special offer.
6. **Personalize:** Avoid generic mailings and tailor each letter to the recipient's needs.
7. **Build lasting relationships:** Promise less and deliver more to create solid bonds with customers.
8. **Test the market**: Try out different approaches and see what works best.
9. **Be accessible:** Avoid formal language and jargon that might put the reader off.
10. **Check everything before sending:** Make sure you have all the necessary resources before starting a direct mail campaign.

12 Steps that must be followed in any persuasive text to generate sales.

1. **Grab attention:** The headline is crucial to capturing the reader's attention right from the start.

2. **Arouse interest:** Present a problem or benefit that is relevant to the reader.
3. **Build desire:** Highlight the benefits of the product or service in an attractive way.
4. **Ask for an action:** Encourage the reader to take action, either by requesting more information or making a purchase.
5. **Provide proof:** Use testimonials or data to back up your claims and increase the reader's confidence.
6. **Present unique advantages:** Highlight what makes your product or service different and better than the competition.
7. **Deal with objections:** Anticipate and respond to the reader's possible questions or concerns.
8. **Create a sense of urgency:** Offer incentives or limited deadlines to motivate immediate action.
9. **Make an irresistible offer:** Make sure that the value offered exceeds the cost perceived by the customer.

10. **Guarantee satisfaction:** Offer guarantees or return policies to reassure the customer.
11. **Close with impact:** Reinforce the benefits and value of the offer and invite the reader to act again.
12. **Revise and improve:** Make a final revision to ensure clarity, cohesion and effectiveness before sending the letter and improve the text with each revision.

We can't overlook the enormous value of a title that catches and holds the reader's attention. In digital marketing, some call this the "headline", which is the first line, the first thing the reader will read. In the case of emails, this refers to the title and also to the first few lines of the email, as mentioned above about the importance of the first paragraph. With one difference, if you are preparing a web sales page, for example, the first phase is the most important one on the page.

Here are 10 examples of headline templates that are proven to grab attention:

1. Finally A 100% Proven Way To Lose *Weight* Without Going On *Crazy Diets!*
2. Learn Now The Only Proven Way To {Speak *English*} {*Only* Studying Online}
3. How {In *Just 3 Days*} I Made *10 Sales* {Without *Investing a Penny in Ads*} - Proven!
4. *{Dermatologist}* Reveals The Secrets To {Having *Pimple-Free Skin*} Without {Having To *Take Medicine!*}
5. Attention: *Pediatricians* Discover How to *Eliminate Newborn Colic Without* Using *Medicine!*
6. Want to Lose *Belly Fat* Without Starving Yourself? Then Follow These 7 *Healthy Habits!*
7. Want to Accelerate *Your Sales?* You Need to Read This First!
8. Wondering How to Make Your *Love Life Better?* Read this!

9. You Need to Generate {More *Sales*} {Through *Facebook?*}

10. {7 *Exercises* You Can Do to *Get a Fit Body* Without Going to the *Gym!*}

You can use what's in brackets {...} to adapt it to your business or niche.

8 Points you need to consider in advance to prepare a persuasive text:

1) **Identify the reader's problem:** Start by highlighting the problem your reader faces. You can sympathize with them or highlight the problem so that they feel its importance.

2. **Offer the solution:** Present your solution to the reader's problem. Show how your product or service effectively solves this problem.

3. **Present your credentials:** Build trust by showing success stories, experience, awards and testimonials from satisfied clients.

4. **Highlight the benefits:** Don't just list the features of your product, but explain how these features directly benefit the reader.

5. **Social proof:** Reinforce your credibility with real testimonials from satisfied customers, preferably with photos and contact information.

6. **Make the final offer:** Present your offer in an attractive way, highlighting the benefits and adding gifts or special conditions if possible.

7. **Promise or guarantee:** Offer a strong guarantee to remove the risk perceived by the customer. Make sure you keep your promise to maintain credibility.

8. **Elements of scarcity:** Create a sense of urgency by informing the reader that the offer is for a limited time or that stocks are limited. This will encourage them to act more quickly.

Examples of offers:

- *"If you buy by this date, (or immediately) you will receive a wonderful gift."*
- *"Our offer is limited to just 50 (products or services) and you will receive them on a first-come, first-served basis. After that, unfortunately, it won't be possible to offer this price."*
- *"This price is only valid for the next 15 days."*

However, once you've made an offer, you won't be able to go back and keep extending the last date. This will cause your customers to lose confidence in you.

To sum up, pay attention to these 3 points when preparing an offer:

1. **Call to action:** Explain clearly how the reader can take advantage of your offer, either by calling you, sending a fax or clicking on a button on the website.

2. **Warning of loss:** Highlight the consequences of not acting now, such as losing the opportunity to receive valuable benefits and seeing competitors excel.

3. **Final reminder:** Include a postscript (PS) to reinforce your offer and remind the reader of the limited time offer, if applicable.

Extra tips:
- List the features and benefits of your product before you start writing.
- Put the sales letter aside for a few days before revising it for a more objective edition.
- Keep a file of examples of successful sales letters for inspiration.
- Create a detailed profile of your target customer to guide your writing.
- Keep the sales letter as engaging as possible, whether it's a short article or a longer e-book, focusing on arousing emotions and encouraging action.

Below are 6 fundamental questions that will help you prepare your persuasive text. Your text must answer these questions to be truly persuasive.

1. **Who are your potential customers?** Before writing, clearly define your target audience in order to target your message effectively. Be specific about who you are trying to reach.

2. **What makes your product or service unique?** Highlight your product's differentials from the competition. Be clear about what makes it special and why customers should choose it.

3. **Why should the customer trust you?** In a market full of false information, build credibility with statistics and testimonials from satisfied customers.

4. **What are the benefits of your product or service?** List all the benefits, both obvious and subtle, that make your offer irresistible to the consumer.

5. **What objections might the customer have?** Anticipate the customer's possible reservations or objections and address them proactively in your sales letter.

6. **Why should the customer act now?** Give the customer a convincing reason to act immediately, such as a special price for a limited time or an exclusive offer. Make sure the urgency is believable and relevant to the customer.

Chapter 5 - Do aesthetics matter for your sales letter?

Is appearance important to you? As for most people, including your customers and leads, the answer is "Yes". In sales especially, appearance plays a key role. For example, in a competitive situation where everything else is equal, a salesperson's visual presentation can be the deciding factor in closing the deal.

Appearance is also crucial to the success of your sales letter.

A marketer with a highly targeted mailing list, a solid offer and well-crafted copy - who also pays careful attention to the appearance of their letter - will certainly get more conversions than someone who focuses solely on content, ignoring aesthetics. The more captivating, the better.

Here are some tips on how to make your sales letter look good:

Tip 1: Always use an easy-to-read font. Most newspapers and magazines use serif fonts for editorial content, such as Times Roman, Courier and Century, which are much more readable than fonts like Arial or Helvetica.

Tip 2: Make your title attractive and keep the opening paragraph short, between one and three lines.

Tip 3: Try to keep the length of your paragraphs between 4 and 6 lines. Your letter should be visually inviting and easy to read. Paragraphs that are too long can discourage the potential customer.

Tip 4: Vary the length of paragraphs to avoid monotony.

Tip 5: Set the body text of your letter in a 10 to 11 point font and use subheadings, bullets and other eye-catching features. Always take the target audience into consideration. If you're writing to young adults, a 10-point font might be appropriate. On the other hand, for a more mature audience, a 14-point font may be more appropriate. Centered subheadings and other visual aids can improve reader engagement.

Subheadings, bulleted lists and other features can give your letter extra appeal and increase response. However, use these features sparingly, as overuse can reduce their overall effectiveness.

Following these 5 tips will attract more attention, keep people reading longer, generate more leads and ultimately close more sales.

Always remember that your letter will be competing with dozens of other sales letters received daily by your potential customers. To stand out, your sales letter needs to be excellent, diverse, professional and relevant.

Do short, powerful sentences increase the impact of your sales letter?

A slogan is a phrase, usually repeated and persuasive, that creates a striking memory, expressing a specific objective or concept. It sticks in the public's mind.

What makes a slogan unforgettable? Conciseness is the first aspect to consider - usually 10 words or less. The slogan must have a specific rhythm.

Thirdly, what are the benefits of using slogans? Brevity, as mentioned earlier, meets the requirements of today's fast pace. Slogans also influence decisions, convince and add reliability. A slogan makes it easier for potential customers to remember and identify a product or service.

Simple, powerful phrases awaken your customers' feelings and lead to an emotional decision to buy. You can increase your sales by using powerful phrases in your marketing emails.

A powerful phrase helps your customer imagine what it will be like to own the product or use the service. It creates an imaginary feeling and motivates your customer to turn that vision into reality. Powerful phrases increase the customer's desire for your product or service and lead to an emotional decision to buy.

Creating a powerful phrase is simple. Start by listing some of the main benefits your customers get from buying from you. Then combine a few highly expressive action words about one or more of these benefits into a short sentence.

Below are some examples of powerful phrases used by different types of businesses:

"Fast! Simple! Affordable!"
"I guarantee you immediate results with my product."

Look at the words used in the two powerful sentences above. They use effective words to create powerful statements.

The most effective power phrases usually combine 3 words or 3 groups of words in a series. Consider, for example:

- "Save time. Save money. Save hassle."
- "Fast! Simple! Affordable!"
- "Enjoy it at home, in the office or in the car"
- "Authority, performance and drive"

Slogans give life, help reinvigorate goals, dreams and even change minds.
There are five main types of slogans:

1. A characteristic: highlighting an exclusivity or difference of a product, substance or object. Example: "Write an ebook in 10 days."
2. A benefit: highlighting the result someone gets, often saving time or money.

3. A question: arousing interest with thought-provoking questions. "How would you like to earn without having to invest a single penny?"

4. A challenge: presenting a challenge to the audience. Example: "The Marines are only looking for a few exceptional men."

5. A structure: describing a design that can be assembled for a specific purpose.

There are 7 ways to make a slogan memorable:

1. make it exciting
2. Be arrogant
3. Self-reference
4. Figurative, playful or humorous
5. Inspiring and motivational
6. To generate painful memories
7. Use of dramatic language

In business, slogans are often used in prospect presentations, websites, email signatures and even in speeches. Be creative, include a slogan in each of your sales and marketing processes and change them regularly if necessary.

Where do you start building slogans? Read through all your notes or materials. Highlight phrases that convey high energy. Rhyming can help create excellent slogans. Read poetry for clues or language that influences and inspires.

Chapter 6 - Why do certain sales letters lose business?

Any consultant can tell you that there are several ways to lose a sale, even when you're confident of winning it. More often than not, the fault lies in the sales letter itself. Most salespeople get excited when customers ask for proposals. After all, it's exciting to have the opportunity to show what you've got, win over the client and close the deal. But creating an impressive proposal is no easy task, and the process takes an enormous amount of time and energy.

Below, we illustrate some of the reasons why a sales letter can lose sales and how to avoid them.

1. avoid creating a text based on a single specific fact.

Some people carry out rigorous research into the client and the project, thinking that this is more than enough. They then draw up their proposal in isolation. However, this is a serious mistake. You can't simply create a proposal unless the client is involved at every stage of the proposal process, including research, objectives, potential benefits, scope, approach and so on.

2. Don't start with your qualifications.

Don't start your proposal with your company's magnificent history. Your customers are interested in what you can actually do for them. Start your main paragraph by focusing on their program, not on how good you are.

3. Don't neglect the executive synopsis.

Many decision-makers are basically concerned with two elements: the executive summary and the price. Surprisingly, some salespeople don't include executive summaries in their proposals. Decision-makers rely on the executive summary to ensure that you understand what they are trying to achieve. If you omit the executive summary, you can be sure that your proposal will be quickly dismissed.

4. Don't just focus on your tools.

Customers only care about the result, not the tools, methods and approaches you will use to achieve the result. Don't talk about how you want to do this and that. Tell them what you can do and in how much time. The "how" can be discussed later, after you get the project.

5. Keep it short and friendly.

Research shows that, given the choice, customers prefer a shorter proposal to a long sales letter full of graphs and drawings. Keep your proposals as concise as possible, but make sure they meet your clients' requirements.

6. Don't use the same CV template.

Every situation is different in some way. So you can't present the same CV to everyone. Prepare different templates. Personalize your CV for each client. Let them know what varied experience you have.

7. Avoid overloading your proposal with jargon.

Most marketing materials are full of jargon and technical terms. This language may be appropriate for textbooks, but it often turns customers off. Try to use simple, clear language.

8. Avoid simple "copy and paste".

To save time, some companies resort to "copy and paste". However, this can lead to disastrous results, such as sending one company's proposal with the name or address of another. Read the proposal carefully before sending it to the client or publishing it on your website. Avoid embarrassment.

9. Be punctual.

Don't try to deceive your customers. If you've missed the deadline for sending the sales proposal, be honest and ask for an extension. Avoid lame excuses.

Chapter 7 - What are the fatal mistakes in email marketing?

To achieve success, your potential customer needs to open, read, believe and act on your sales letter. To do this, you need to arouse interest and generate desire for your product or service.

An effective sales letter should achieve the same result as a successful salesperson. However, just like a salesperson, the sales letter must also avoid certain mistakes.

Here are some common fatal mistakes made in most marketing emails:

Fatal mistake #1 - Avoiding using a mass mailing approach.

Sending your sales letter as a mass mailing can turn recipients off. As soon as they realize it's one of those mass emails, they're likely to discard it. Writing your letter with a generic mindset, rather than focusing on each reader individually, undermines your letter's ability to establish a real bond with the reader. A sales letter is an individual marketing tool, so make it as personal as possible.

Fatal mistake #2 - Avoiding writing long, boring letters.

A letter doesn't have to be long to look long; it's the content that matters. Even a one-page letter can seem long if it's monotonous. People are willing to consume long content if it's interesting. If you go on in a boring way, you run the risk of being ignored. Offer your product or service properly at a fair price and present it in an interesting way. Half the battle is won.

Fatal mistake #3 - Not sticking to formal, grammatically correct language.

Writing a sales letter is not like writing a school essay. You should use more common and informal language to make it easier to read. You may have to break some grammar rules to do so. The basic aim of a sales letter is to generate sales, not to get an A in grammar.

Fatal mistake #4 - Not allowing the reader to make excuses for not reading your letter.

Nobody cares who you are or what you offer. People are only interested in how you can benefit them. So you need to grab the reader's attention in the first 20 seconds or so. Start with a provocative phrase or slogan and try to appeal to the emotions. Your aim should be to keep the potential customer's attention.

Fatal mistake #5 - Not establishing your credibility correctly.

The evidence you offer in your sales letter to support your pedigree can take many forms. For example, include testimonials from satisfied customers, preferably in the form of stories, and add photos to increase credibility. Many readers don't care to check, but including details such as names, addresses and telephone numbers increases reliability.

Chapter 8 - What are the pitfalls of a "what if" approach?

"If I could show you how you can save money, even without reducing your daily expenses?"
"What if I told you that you could increase your market share in three months?"
"What if I could help you lose weight quickly?"

If you are a potential consumer who has heard these "false" statements before, you are unlikely to feel motivated to buy.

Planned sales practices are rarely successful when it comes to dealing with customer objections and have no place in the world of effective sales.

The genuine method involves dealing with your potential customer's objections during the sales process itself. This means asking the right questions from the start and tailoring your product or service to solve their problem.

It's true that many people will have objections when buying your products or services. The best way to deal with this is to investigate their real needs, assess their problems and offer a product or service that really benefits them. To do this, you need to dedicate a good amount of time to them.

You need to ask high-quality questions that make your client think. This may sound easy, but in practice it's complicated, because it's challenging to ask questions that really make people think. Many salespeople perceive these questions as personal and imagine that customers won't be enthusiastic about answering them.

It's important to remember that most people respond well to challenging questions and that this increases your standing in their eyes.

You can ask questions like:
- What are your short-term goals?
- How do you intend to achieve these goals?
- What challenges do you face in achieving these goals?

The basic aim of these questions is to find out what problem the customer is facing and how you and your product or service can help solve it.

We can't ignore the truth. Today's buyers are more demanding than ever and have probably heard all the lines similar to what you want to say. They don't like clichéd, traditional or manipulative approaches.

Most people have specific objections when making a purchasing decision. Sales are closed when the buyer recognizes the value of your product or service, or when you prove to be an expert capable of helping them solve a problem.

Just asking "What if I could" is not a successful approach. It's cliché and rarely works these days.

Chapter 9 - What do you do when you just can't write a sales letter?

You need to write a sales letter, but the words just won't come. You think, think and think, but you don't succeed. So what do you do now?

It's a really frustrating situation and it can happen to any of us at some point. But there's a great way to get your creativity flowing.

Are you really aware of your product?
Suppose you're selling a treadmill. You really need to know how to use it. When can you use it? What are the limitations and side effects?

Knowing and caring about your product gives you the passion to tell the whole world about it. To praise it. To love it. To show it off.

So now the first block has been overcome. Now that you know the product and have fallen in love with it, you can chatter away to describe it.

Then record the reasons and how it will help you, if any. Will it make my life easier? Will it add value? Will it solve a problem? Also, is it too expensive? It's too ugly and so on.

List everything: the good, the bad and even the ugly.

You need to find out why people will buy from you.

What is so unique about your product or service? The best way to do this is to debate.

Soon, you'll have so many opinions that you won't be able to keep up. Just keep going until you've exhausted all the ideas.

When you've finished, just take a look at what you've written and make a list of all the spectacular ideas you have. List them in order of priority.

Now you have a draft of your letter.

Use the most significant basis of the list, the main reason for someone to buy your product, and turn it into a wonderful headline.

Allow the ideas on the list to appear in your sales letter by using subheadings or highlights when you need to emphasize a point. Soon, your letter will have almost written itself.

In conclusion, when writing your letter, remember to write it to only one person at a time. Do something special!

Chapter 10 - The difference between a sales letter and an advertisement

People often confuse the functions of the advertisement and the sales letter. Both aim to win new customers or sell a product or service, but there are significant differences in their approach.

A sales letter is a more individualized form of advertising than an advertisement. While thousands or even millions of people can see an advertisement in a magazine or newspaper, a sales letter is directed only at the eyes of the intended recipient. Even though sales letters are often sent out in large quantities, the recipient still perceives them as more personal than an advertisement in a printed publication.

Unlike an advertisement, a sales letter takes a more personal, informal and welcoming approach. This creates a closer and more natural tone, allowing the recipient to get a better sense of the sender's character, interest and seriousness.

Having your reader's attention is fundamental

For any marketing professional, attention is a valuable resource. With consumers being bombarded with thousands of advertising messages every day, the challenge is to make your message stand out from the crowd and be taken seriously.

An effective sales letter needs to achieve two goals:

1. Ensure that the potential client reads the letter to the end.
2. Motivate the potential customer to take the desired action.

If the marketer can't achieve the first stage, the second will be impossible.

Many marketers invest in making the sales letter envelope attractive because they know that half the battle is won if the recipient opens the letter.

For online marketers, where there are no physical envelopes, strategies such as creating flash images can be used to attract the attention of the target audience.

Tips for attracting attention:

1. Use a RED headline, as tests have shown that it stands out more than other font colors. Red is associated with danger, but it also conveys the message: "This is important. Read me!"

2. Eliminate elements from the page that do not contribute to the sales message or are distracting. This includes animated graphics and intense background colors that compete with the text in the foreground. Simplicity, such as black font on a white background, works well. Limiting the use of colors to

three or fewer also makes the document more reader-friendly.

3. Avoid making the text too long, as this can make reading monotonous. Long lines require a lot of eye and head movement.

4. The title should be catchy and appear prominently.

5. Use attractive formatting and design in the sales letter, such as highlighting, bold, bullets and appropriate subheadings to make it easier to read.

6. Make the letter inviting and visually appealing.

7. Encourage the reader to continue reading throughout the letter. Keep their interest alive.

8. Be unique. If all the sales letters in your sector are similar, why should a potential

customer read yours? Use mascots, humor, cartoons and other elements to stand out.

9. Focus your message on the reader, not on your company or product. Many companies make the mistake of focusing on themselves, but the customer is interested in their own wants and needs. They need to know how your product or service will benefit them.

A quick lesson in writing lucid sales letters:

The type of sales letter that gets read, improves sales and keeps the reader's interest until the last word usually has to do with the conversational tone adopted. You want the reader to feel as if they are talking to a friend who is giving them advice on something interesting and useful.

How to generate a conversational tone:

1. Use succinct sentences, as you would when talking to a friend. Avoid long, complex sentences.

2. Use descriptive word pictures to create vivid images in the reader's mind. Fully describe what you are offering.
3. Write authentically and directly, as if you were talking from the heart to the heart.
4. Talk to your potential client in their language, avoiding professional jargon and mentioning things they can relate to.

Tips for formatting your sales letter to improve its effectiveness:

- Use a catchy headline at the top of the page, in red for greater prominence.
- Include your name at the beginning and end of the sales text, as well as your scanned signature.
- Use subheadings in red to highlight important sections.
- Highlight testimonials from satisfied customers in separate boxes, using a different color if possible.

- Avoid using red to highlight the price, as it can give the impression of stopping. Reserve that color for the headline.
- Make sure that the bonuses offered are related to the main offer.
- Use white space to rest the reader's eyes and make the letter easier to read.
- Choose a legible and attractive font and text color.
- Always include a specific call to action, indicating to the potential customer the action you want them to take.

Chapter 11 - Does a text need to be long or short to be persuasive?

The most important factor is to be interesting. If the letter manages to hold the reader's attention, it can be effective, regardless of its length, whether it's one page or several.

Studies show that a long, interesting sales letter generally converts more potential customers into buyers. This is because a long letter manages to create a relationship with the reader over time, evoking a feeling of companionship and trust.

It is crucial that the letter identifies with the readers and shows empathy with their problems. This creates a sense of trust, leading readers to believe that you understand their problems and can offer a solution.

What's more, a personalized sales letter for each potential customer is more effective than a generic approach. It shows that you are genuinely interested in helping the customer, which can lead to a relationship of trust and even the recommendation of your product or service to others.

So long, interesting copy can be an effective strategy for a sales letter.

Do I need to be a grammar teacher or a professional copywriter to write a persuasive text? What if there are some grammatical errors in my text?

Although writing is important, it goes beyond "real writing". The presentation of the information and the formatting of the letter play a significant role in the effectiveness of the message.

For example, consider a situation in which a letter full of grammatical and spelling mistakes announces that the reader has been selected to win a major prize. Despite the errors, the content of the message overcomes the linguistic flaws, making the recipient extremely happy. This demonstrates that, in some situations, the clarity of the message and the way it resonates with the audience can be more important than grammatical perfection.

On the other hand, imagine that I write an impeccable letter on high-quality paper. No spelling or grammar mistakes. I've even sprayed on a little perfume. But at the end of the day, I'm doing my best to sell an old dilapidated building on the outskirts. Do you care now? Oh, no.

It's not so much how you write as what you say.

The bottom line is: there may be exceptions, but the truth is that if you focus on sending your proposals to people who have already shown an interest in products or services similar to yours, with a truly irresistible offer, your chances of closing the deal will be much higher than if you just approached uninterested people with a perfectly worded sales letter.

The monster of a sales letter

All too often, marketers create their own monsters (like Dr. Frankenstein) in their marketing emails. They start in the wrong place, mix up information and confuse the reader.

Sales letters work best when you have something to offer. Basically, it comes down to questions like these: What can you do for me? Why should I spend my time reading your letter? Quick... convince me that I need your product or service.

When creating a better sales letter, start by using the right head, instead of using the wrong head like our Dr. Frankenstein. In other words, use a good headline, start well. The first few lines are super important.

The right title can make all the difference to your sales letter. Stay focused on your target market. Tackle a big problem that your audience faces (if you have the answer). If you can play with words in a clever way, go for it; but if that's not your style, keep it simple. There's no perfect length for a headline, but avoid the wrong words and keep it short. The aim is to make them think of you.

Once you've grabbed the reader's attention with the title, don't let it slip away. The PS is crucial, so don't fill it with unnecessary words. Say something that will encourage them to read the letter from the start.

The first paragraph is vital. Get straight to the point and show the main benefit of your offer. If you engage the reader here, the rest of the letter can answer questions and address concerns.

Fill the body of the letter with benefits, not just features. Speak the language of your audience, be informal and clear. Use humor sparingly to avoid misunderstandings.

People are busy, so grab their attention with bold and highlights. Highlight important information to keep them interested.

After talking about your products or services, show them why they should trust you. Testimonials from satisfied customers help establish your credibility.

Once you've addressed any doubts, offer a satisfaction guarantee. This will reduce the customer's hesitation to buy.

After writing, take some time before revising. Test your letter on the market and adjust as necessary.

Remember to keep track of the responses and continue with your marketing efforts.

Print quality is important. Use a good quality printer and paper to ensure a good presentation.

Keep to a budget. Don't skimp on poor quality paper and ink, as this will affect the reader's impression. The content of the letter is the most important thing, but a good presentation increases the chances of it being read.

Good sales letters are really good salespeople.

Let's analyze 10 points that confirm this thesis:

1. Self-inspired: Just like the best salespeople, a good sales letter should be self-sufficient, offering all the details needed to close the sale.

2. Tested and refined: Just as salespeople learn from their mistakes, sales letters must also be tested and refined to ensure effectiveness.

3. Adapting to Pressure: As salespeople must adapt to distractions and pressures, a sales letter must capture the customer's attention and keep it even in the midst of other distractions.

4. Efficient communication: Just as salespeople need to communicate in a clear and friendly way, sales letters should be simple and easy to understand.

5. Energy and Vitality: An effective sales letter should convey energy and enthusiasm, just like an energetic salesperson.

6. Organization and discipline: A good sales letter must be well organized and disciplined in its approach.

7. Teamwork: In some cases, a sales letter works in conjunction with other marketing tools, and it is important that the tone and message are aligned.

8. Attention to the customer: Despite being a one-sided conversation, a sales letter should feel like a two-way conversation, conveying human warmth.

9. Seriousness and Commitment: Only send a sales letter when you are committed to keeping your promises.

10. Closed questions: Just as salespeople use specific questions to guide the conversation, a good sales letter can include closed questions to direct the reader to a specific conclusion.

So it's true that a good sales letter shares many qualities with a good salesperson.

Yes, this technique is useful for directing the conversation towards a more efficient closing of the deal. Specific questions such as "Do you realize you have a problem?" or "Will you make this decision in a fortnight?" can help elicit clear answers that lead to closing the sale. It's important to ask them in a friendly and respectful tone, avoiding any pressure on the customer. This shows consideration and maintains credibility, which is fundamental to the success of the negotiation.

Chapter 12 - The ten basic rules for writing a good sales letter

For many small businesses, a sales letter is the only marketing tool available due to budget constraints. However, a well-crafted sales letter can have a significant impact on the bottom line. Following a few simple guidelines can boost profits and sales results. Here is a brief summary for your notes and recaps:

1. Focus on the customer: Before you write, put yourself in the customer's shoes. They want to know what they get out of your offer.
2. Be Personal: Write as if you were talking to a friend, not a crowd.
3. Highlight Benefits: Sell the benefits, not just the features of the product or service.
4. Capture Attention: Be captivating from the start to compete with other emails.
5. Be Specific: Offer relevant and specific information, without beating around the bush.

6. Talk to the Customer: Maintain a friendly, conversational tone.
7. Test and Adjust: See if the card would convince you to buy.
8. Size Matters: Don't worry about size, as long as it's interesting.
9. Attention to Appearance: Use fonts and designs that are easy to read, and divide up the text to make it easier to read.
10. Direct the Action: Tell the reader clearly what to do next, don't leave them guessing.

These basic rules can help you create an effective and persuasive sales letter.

Chapter 13 - Five useful secrets of an effective sales letter

It's true, the crucial difference between an average sales letter and an effective one is the result it produces. Writing a successful sales letter is not as complicated as it sounds. By following a few simple tips and guidelines, you can create a sales letter that brings exceptional results.

Here are five more secrets to writing a sales letter that rocks:

1. Devote a few hours a day to studying highly effective marketing emails. Look at the details, such as headlines and paragraph structure. Analyze the style and organization to learn important nuances.

2. Compile the best sales letters you can find and create a notebook with them. When you're writing your own letter, refer to this notebook for inspiration. Don't copy

directly; instead, extract ideas and adapt them to your own words.

3. Do thorough research on your potential customers to understand their desires, needs, dreams and motivations. The more personalized your sales letter, the more impact it will have. Knowing your target audience is fundamental to success.

4. After researching your potential customers, take some time to relax. Forget about everything for a day or two before you start writing. This allows you to come back to work with a fresh and practical mind.

5. Test your sales letter by sending it to several potential customers. Observe the results and adjust as necessary. Testing is the only way to determine whether your letter is really effective. If it doesn't work, revise and try again until you get the results you want.

If you're disappointed with the results of your sales letter, there's a simple and powerful solution: emotion. Buying decisions are influenced by emotion, so your letter needs to connect emotionally with the reader to encourage them to act. Two main forces are at play: the promise of gain and the fear of losing.

So how do you add emotion to your sales letter? Here are some simple tips:

1) Touch the pain: Identify the reader's problem and highlight how it affects their life. Show how they are struggling and unable to achieve their goals. Make the problem seem bigger than it is.

2) Use stories: Stories are powerful for arousing emotions. Tell stories that generate expectations of success, avoid problems or make dreams come true. Also share stories of people who didn't use your product and suffered the consequences, increasing the fear of missing out.

3) Use emotional words: Choose words that arouse strong feelings. Get to know your audience and use words that affect them emotionally, such as "money", "success", "making dreams come true".

Remember, your sales letter should highlight the benefits of your product or service, solve the customer's problems and build trust right from the start. Don't forget to apply emotion sensibly and ethically. Put yourself in your customer's shoes and ask yourself how you would react. And remember, always test your marketing strategy to achieve the best possible result.

Avoiding certain words in a sales letter can make all the difference between a successful sale and a failure. Here are some words you should avoid at all costs:

1) "Buy": Avoid directly asking people to buy. This can put them off. Instead, use terms like "receive" or "invest".

2) "Learn": This word can remind people of times of study and effort. Instead, use "discover" to convey information in a more attractive way.

3) "Tell": Instead of simply "telling", use "revealing" to create more impact and interest.

4) "Things": This word can make your letter monotonous. Replace it with "tips", "tricks" or "techniques" to keep the reader's interest.

5) "Bonus": Instead of just mentioning a "bonus", highlight what the customer will receive in a more attractive way, such as "fabulous gifts".

Choosing the right words can significantly increase the effectiveness of your sales letter by activating the buying emotion in your potential customers.

It's important to carefully examine the words used in a sales letter, especially when it comes to get-rich-quick ventures. For example, the expression "turnkey" may imply that the deal is ready to run without any additional effort on the part of the client, but this is often not the case. You often have to install software, learn and work to get results.

In addition, it is crucial to watch out for the use of the words "could" and "get rich quick". It is ethical and transparent to realistically report potential earnings, rather than promising instant riches. Misleading customers with exaggerated promises may generate an immediate response, but in the long term it damages credibility and trust.

The success of a sales letter depends on the words you choose and how you use them to achieve your goal. You don't need to be a professional copywriter to write an effective sales letter; the important thing is to use simple, friendly and conversational language.

Creating a genuine connection with your audience can be achieved in a number of ways:

1. Yes questions: In marketing emails, use questions that lead to positive answers, such as "You realize the value of this, right?" or "Don't you deserve the best?" This encourages your prospect to agree with you and act as suggested.
2. Genuine testimonials: Include testimonials from satisfied customers to increase the perceived value of your product or service. Make sure the testimonials are authentic to build trust with your audience.
3. Mirroring: Adapt to your client's language, tone and communication style. For example, adapt your

approach when talking to a doctor, accountant or event manager to create a stronger connection.

Building a connection is essential to establishing credibility and trust with your target audience. When your audience feels connected and understood by you, they are more likely to trust you and your products or services.

Chapter 14 - Final Summary

To ensure that your sales letter is effective and engaging, here is a final checklist:

1. Personalization: Use the potential customer's name and title to create an immediate connection.

2. Friendly and special tone: Make the letter welcoming and unique to capture the reader's attention.

3. Jokes, slogans and eye-catching headlines: Use stories, impactful phrases and eye-catching headlines to grab interest right from the start.

4. Natural language: Write as you speak and proofread aloud to ensure clarity and fluency.

5. Simplicity: Keep paragraphs short and use simple language that resonates with the target audience.

6. Practical editing: Set the letter aside for a while before revising it for more objective editing.

7. External feedback: Ask friends and family for an outside perspective before sending the letter.

8. Visual presentation: Opt for an attractive format, such as colored paper, and use a friendly font.

9. Calls to action: Include clear instructions on what the reader should do next and highlight special offers.

10. Credibility: Reinforce your offer with genuine testimonials and a satisfaction guarantee to increase customer confidence.

11. Direct contact: Include a reply card, telephone number or URL to facilitate contact.

12. Brevity: Keep the letter concise and to the point to avoid overwhelming the reader.

13. Creativity: Experiment with irregular formats or visual elements to increase curiosity and the open rate.

14. Personalized segmentation: If possible, manually address each envelope or e-mail for a more personalized approach.

15. Avoid commercial logos: Don't distinguish the envelope with commercial logos to increase the likelihood of opening.

By following these tips and ensuring a careful approach, your sales letter will have a better chance of achieving the desired success and generating positive results for your company.

Now that you're familiar with all aspects of creating an effective sales letter, let's summarize other important points:

1) Inspire hope: Show how your product or service can make the customer's life more convenient and comfortable, creating a sense of hope in what you offer.

2. Create urgency: Add incentives to the offer to motivate customers to act quickly by highlighting stock shortages or the limited validity of the offer.

3. Establish authority: Demonstrate knowledge and expertise on the subject, conveying trust and credibility in the eyes of customers.

4. Be impartial: Avoid appearing to be pressuring customers to buy. Instead, show that you are offering genuine and impartial help to solve their problems.

5. Use fear persuasively: Identify the customer's problems and concerns and show how your product or service can help them overcome them, emphasizing the benefits of acting now.

6. Highlight your uniqueness: Set yourself apart from the competition by highlighting the exclusive benefits of your product or service and even suggesting that customers try other options before deciding.

Creating an effective sales letter is fundamental to the success of any business. Even if you're not a talented writer, you can achieve positive results by learning to communicate the benefits of your product or service in a persuasive way.

Now that you have all the information you need, put these tips into practice to create an engaging sales letter that keeps customers interested and ultimately generates profits for your business.

Don't forget mental triggers and try to be more of a friend than a salesperson. With this information in mind, start your persuasive texts and good business!

www.ingramcontent.com/pod-product-compliance
Lightning Source LLC
Chambersburg PA
CBHW070306230526
45470CB00002B/752